YOU…

Carter Remy

Copyright © 2020 by Carter Remy

This book is copyright. All rights are reserved.

No part of this publication may be used, reproduced, distributed, or transmitted in any format whatsoever without prior written permission of the author or publisher, except in the case of quotations in reviews and certain noncommercial uses permitted by copyright laws.

ISBN: 9798585868290
Imprint: Independently published
Print copyright: © 2020 Kindle Direct Publishing.
Content Copyright: © 2020 Carter Remy

YOU…

Your lips

Perfectly rounded.
Evenly spacious.
Very well-manicured and balanced.
Cosmically basking in rays of light.
Its saturation is enough to perpetuate the heart
causing it to pulsate and quiver uncontrollably.
Never in need of attention but,
its submerged and drenched enunciated physiognomy
annunciate itself so eloquently.

Your lips are unlike any other.

C.R.

The ropes

The notion of them makes you acquiescent,
the sight of them makes you compliant.
Your body, already pulsating, begging for just a slight
caress with them.
You've given in, given up control,
you're more than ready to accept your dominant's
erogenous orders that are sure to leave you drenched.

It's just something about those ropes huh?

C.R.

The color red

Why must you wear it so submissively?
Paired up with your emotive yet picturesque scarlet heels,
making every one of your steps ever so enticing.
Why must you make it drift so seductively?
Leaving its flirtatious linger to enthrall.
Why must you accessorize it with such controlled
compulsion, often signaling a salacious tryst?

You now have made red to be my favorite color.

C.R.

Let me help you

Let me help you uncover your celestial body.
Perfectly structured and very much aesthetically symmetrical,
let me help you get to where every single one of your orgasmic squeals is a submission to my questions.
Let me help you explore your body and its nature as it takes a mental photograph from my tongue's recreational entertainment between your lower lips.

Just,
Let me help you.

C.R.

Mine

You are no longer in control.
Your decisions are now mine.
Your service will be to please.
It'll be rewarded but will also be swiftly punished even with the slightest offense.
You're not to regard me as none other but as instructed.
I must prompt you to adhere to your submissive nature and total devotion, which will lead you to heed to nothing but our shared desires.
Though novel to you, this is now your way of life.
Abide by them and cherished them through every endeavor allowing them to yield their continuous dominant nature.

You are now mine.

C.R.

Your throat

My hand now lives there.
It is the epicenter of my dominance.
Though soft and fragile, it is the very spot that makes your breath expire with obedience.
It is the purest form of communication, one of which does not allow you to refuse me.
Your understanding of self has never been so clear until you felt my whisper telling you that you...now belong to me.

C.R.

No one told me

No one told me what fucking you would be like.
It's midnight.
And we are under the covers of my sheets, scarfing down
the savory taste of each other's body.

Looking at the beautifully carved shape of your lips,
I started to think about how the two of us would penetrate
each other's souls.

I started to dream about how your hips would move in a wave-like motion with every stroke as you take me on a ride in your ocean.

With a glance,
I noticed how such a well-manicured posture began to engrave itself in numerical values within the pools of my memories.

Your touch is so invigorating that a picturesque current traveled through every single cell of my body.
For just a brief moment, the lack of air in your moans synced our bodies.

You became the hydrogen to my oxygen, and with the two of us combined, our thirst would soon be quenched.

You undressed not only my body but also my pineal gland.

Two can play that game.
In turn, I made you wonder and question your very
emotional state as to whether or not I fucked you so right
to the point I took a piece of your insanity.

Gasping for air,
you sang loudly as you can.
Screaming not only my name,
but spelling backwardly every letter that makes up the English alphabet.

We've moved on from positions to positions,
and every time, I am marveled at the way you flip your hair.
Like a goddess, gently, you positioned your fingers on my chest.
Slowly you glide the tip of your nails through my body as if you were taking a mental photograph.

No one told me what fucking you
would be like

    C.R.

You…

www.ingramcontent.com/pod-product-compliance
Lightning Source LLC
Chambersburg PA
CBHW070846220526
45466CB00002B/902